Design
Elements 1

Design
Elements 1

A Visual Reference by
Richard Hora
Mies Hora

The Art Direction Book Company, New York

Dedicated to Helena
and to all those who utilize this book.

Book design by Richard and Mies Hora
Special thanks to
Don Barron and David C. Levy
for their generous assistance.

Art Direction Book Company
10 East 39th Street
New York, New York 10016

Library of Congress Catalog Card Number 81–66127
International Standard Book Number 0–910158–72–X

Forward

The design elements in this collection are all arranged for your convenience. The material was selected from a wide variety of sources, both old and new, with many created specifically for this volume. It is organized into specific categories to speed search-and-find. Each design element was carefully selected for quality and general usefulness. All are generously sized for reproduction purposes. This book represents over forty years of collection and use, beginning as a working tool and eventually developing into a labor of love. We hope you find *Design Elements 1* to be the inspirational and easy-to-use source file that we intended.

Richard Hora
Mies Hora

Introduction

Visual symbols are among the oldest
permanent means of communication,
dating back some 30,000 years to the caves
of Lascaux and Altamira. Our ancestors
included the shapes of arrows, hands, and
geometric forms in their representations
of bulls, horses and mammoths. Clearly
those images fulfill some architypal human
need. Despite the distances we have
travelled from those caves, we find that
these same forms remain a compelling
means for transmitting information. They
are, today as then, an indispensable part
of our visual language. In recent years we
have seen this tradition enriched by the
signs of modern life—television screens,
filmstrips, scientific nomenclature, etc.

The availability of a resource in which the
very best of these images have been
selected and exquisitely rendered for the
purposes of reproduction is a great service
to all of us, but it is most important to
designers. The painstaking care with which
Richard and Mies Hora have undertaken
this task is reflected in this series of books,
which represent an enormous research
effort as well as the exercise of astute
judgement, taste and skill. Here is a very
high level of visual quality and design
utility. The thoughtfulness and comprehen-
sive nature of their work makes this series
invaluable for the concerned designer.

David C. Levy, Ph.D.
Executive Dean
Parsons School of Design

Contents

Targets
Concentric Circles
Circles
Spirals
Whirls
Pinwheels
Rotors
Optical Designs
Gears
Radials
Asterisks

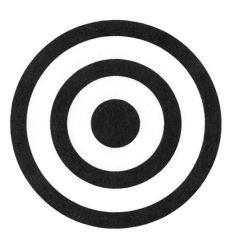

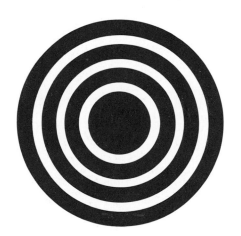

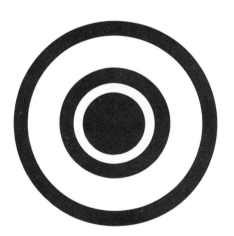

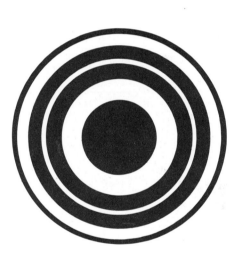

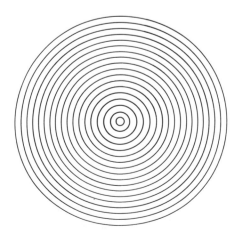

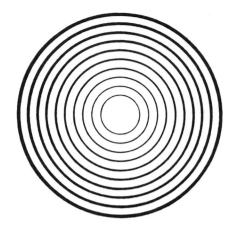

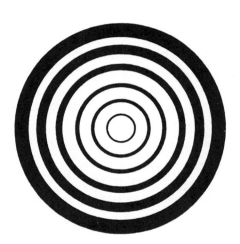

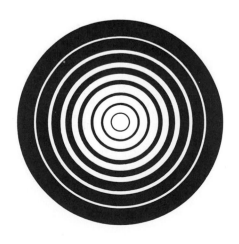

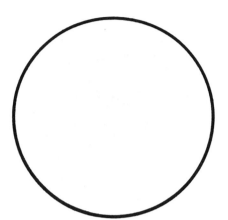
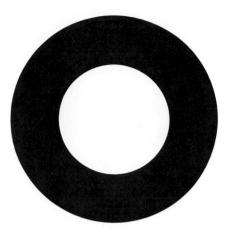
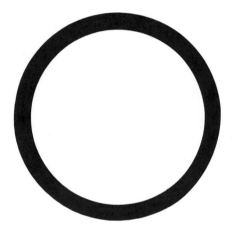

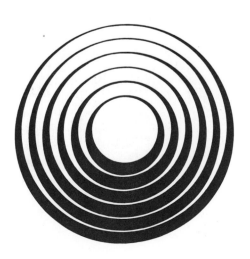

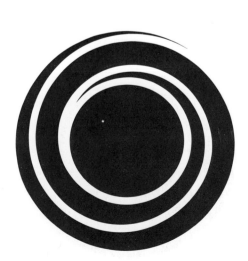

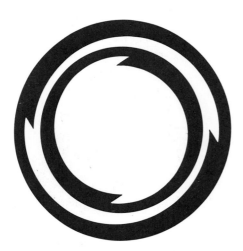

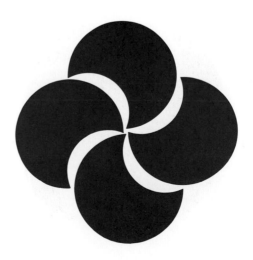

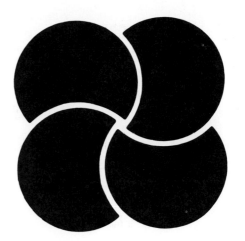

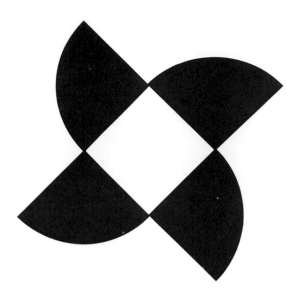

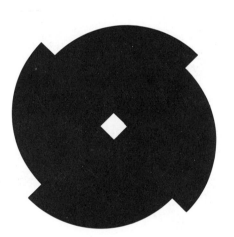

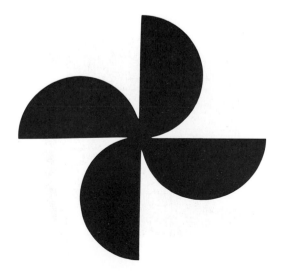

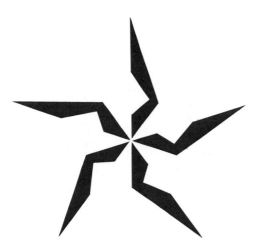

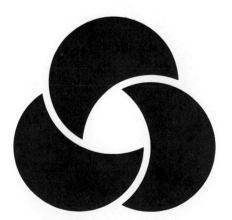
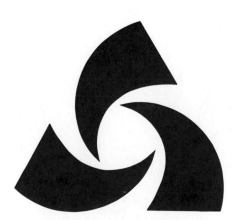

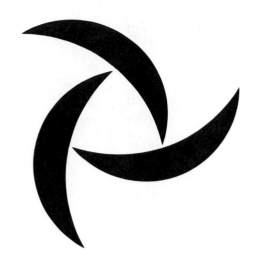

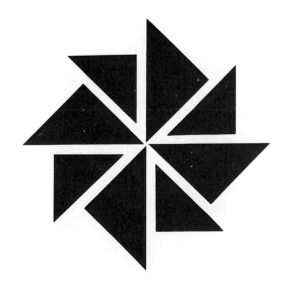

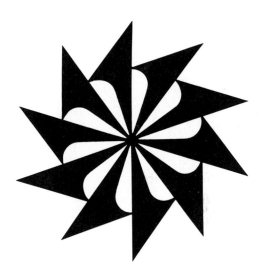

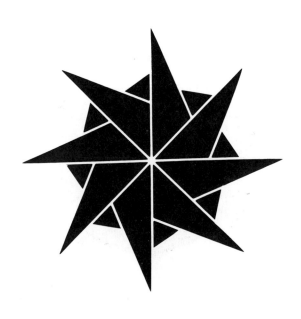

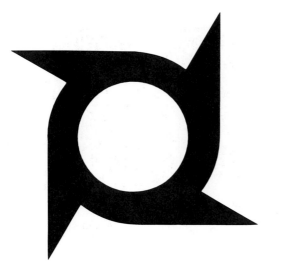

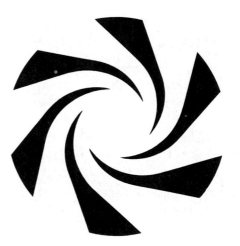

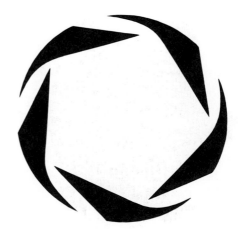

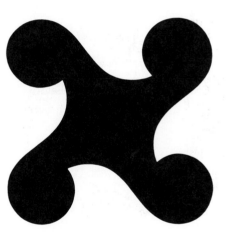

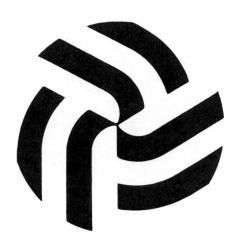

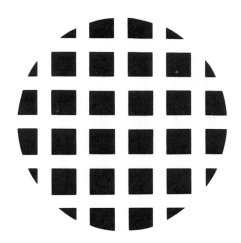

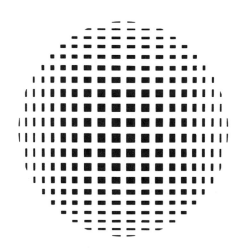

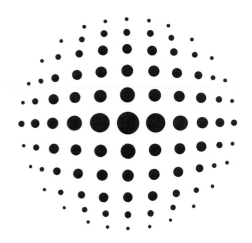

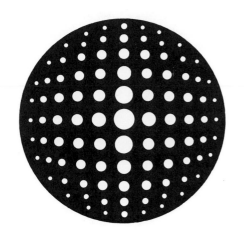

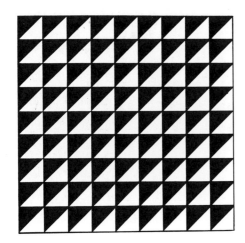

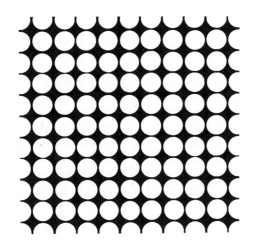

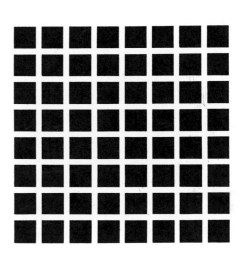

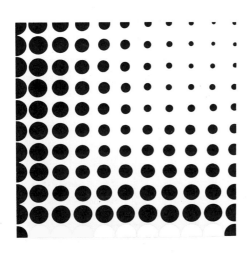

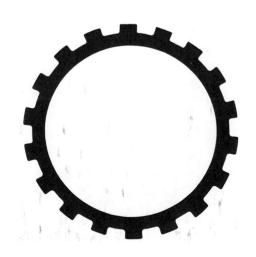

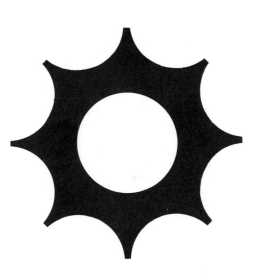

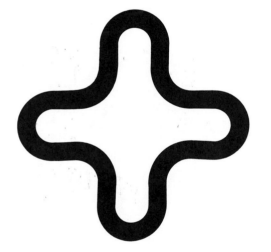

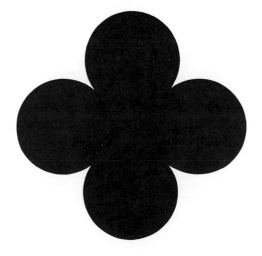

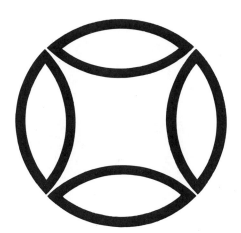

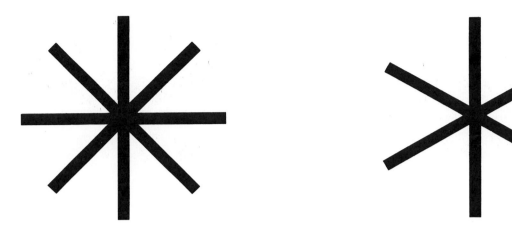

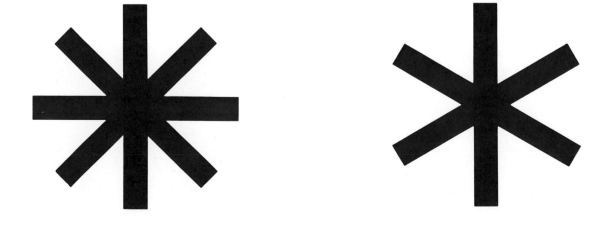

Stars (five-pointers)
Stars (variations)
Compass Faces

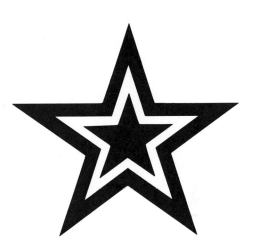

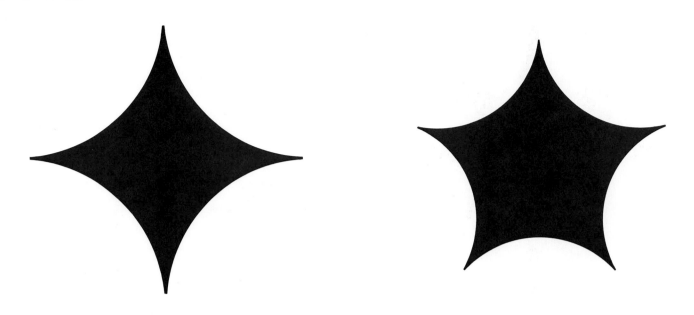

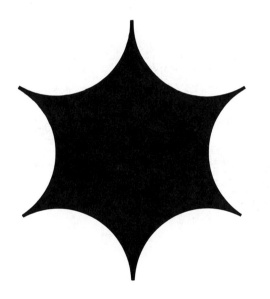

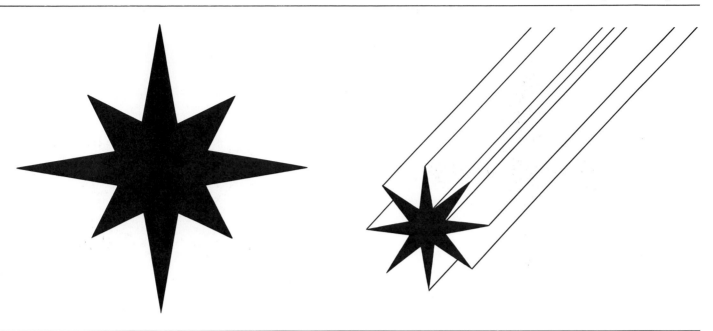

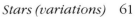

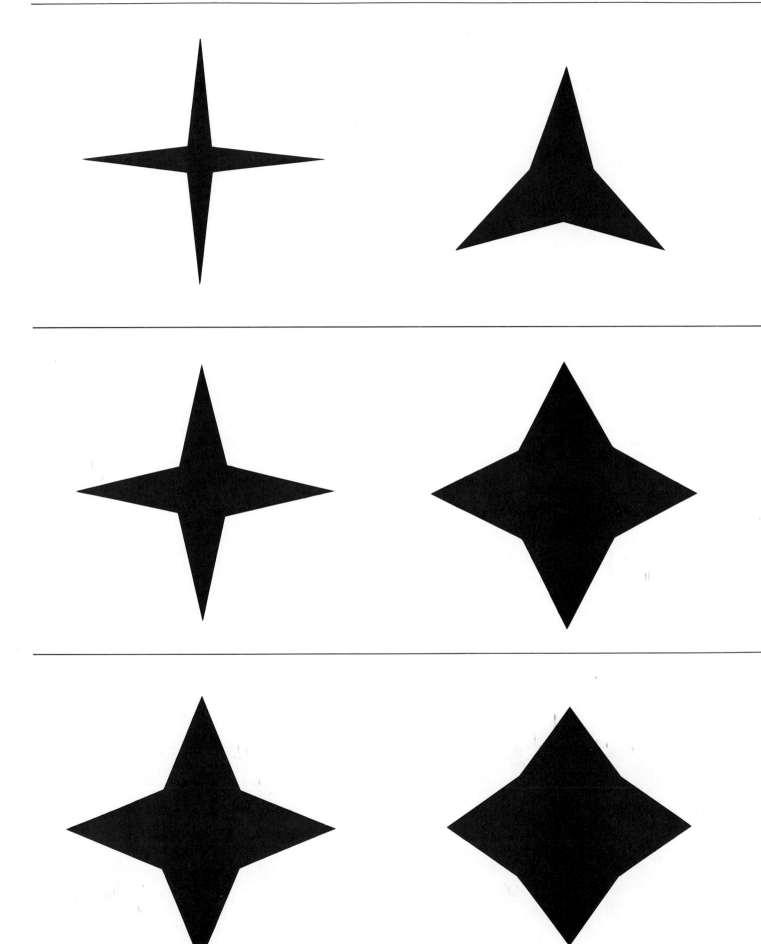

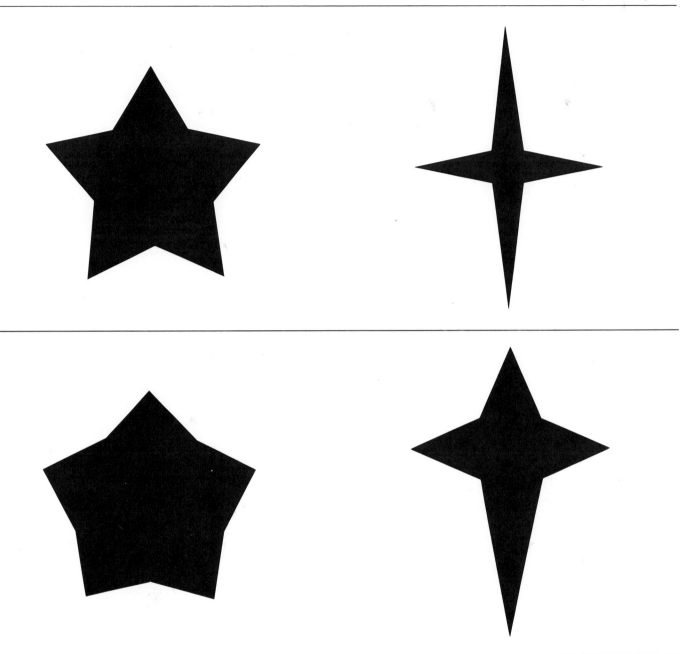

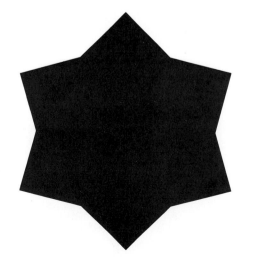

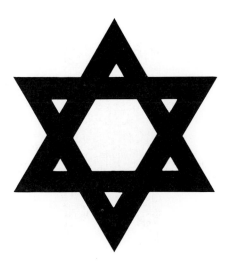

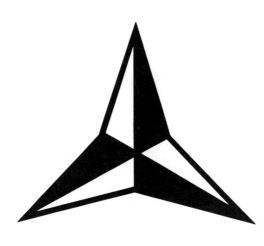

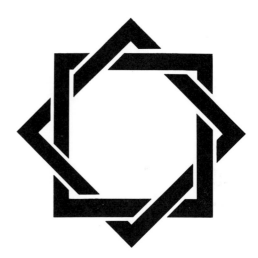

Solar Shapes
Sun Faces
Moons
Moon Phases (1-30)

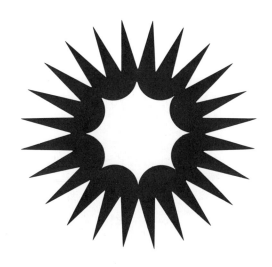

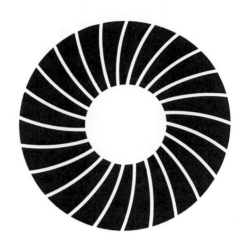

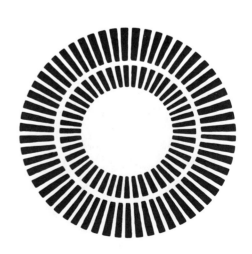

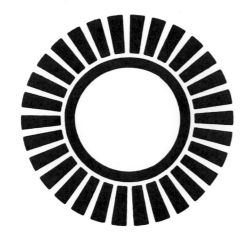

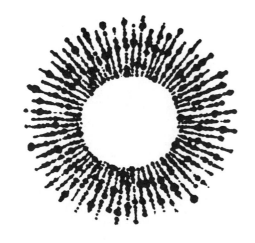

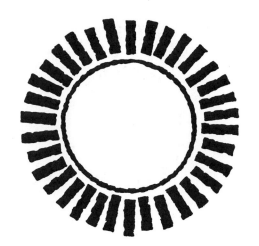

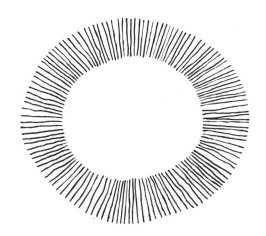

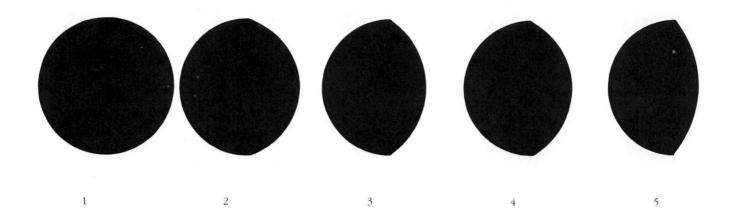

1   2   3   4   5

11   12   13   14   15

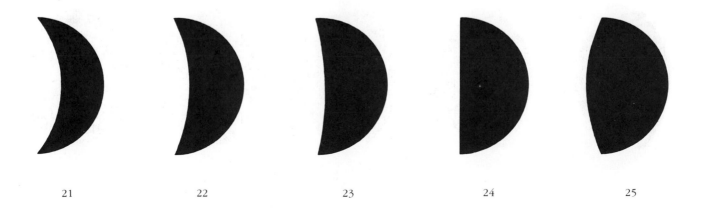

21   22   23   24   25

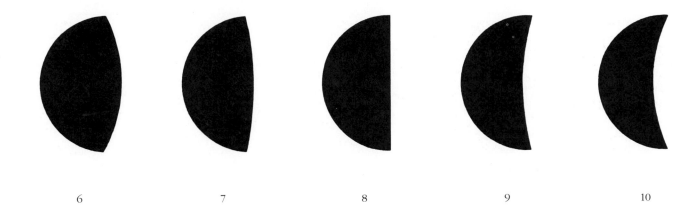

6	7	8	9	10

16	17	18	19	20

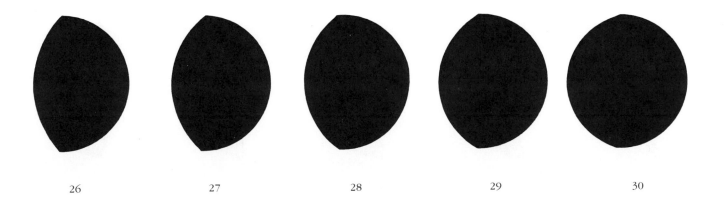

26	27	28	29	30

TV Screens
Cartouches/Tablets, etc.
Ellipses/Ovals
Shields
Triangles

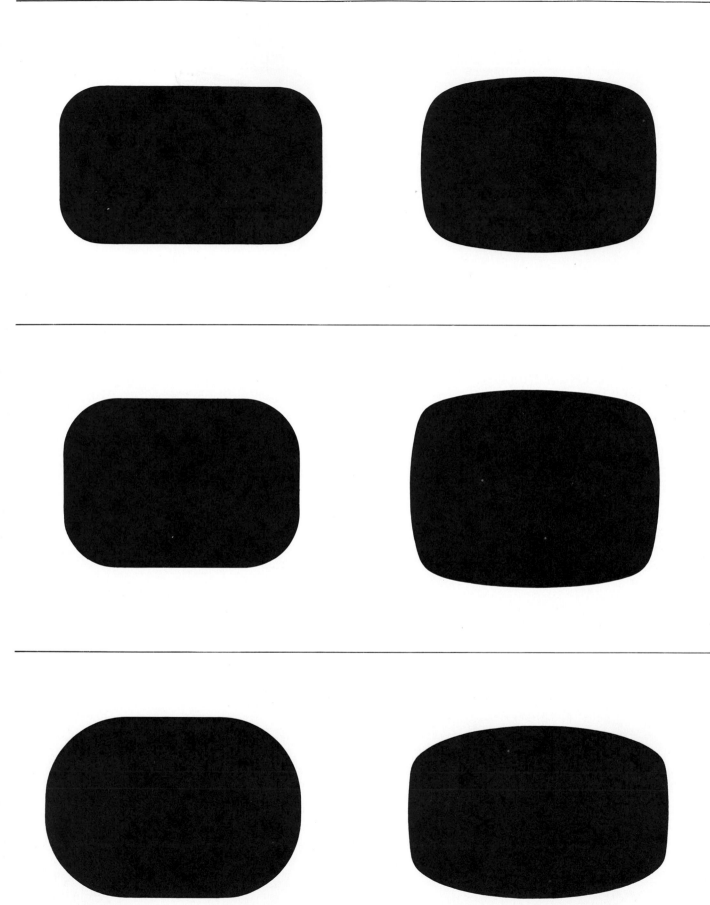

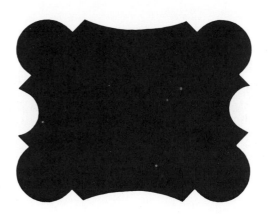

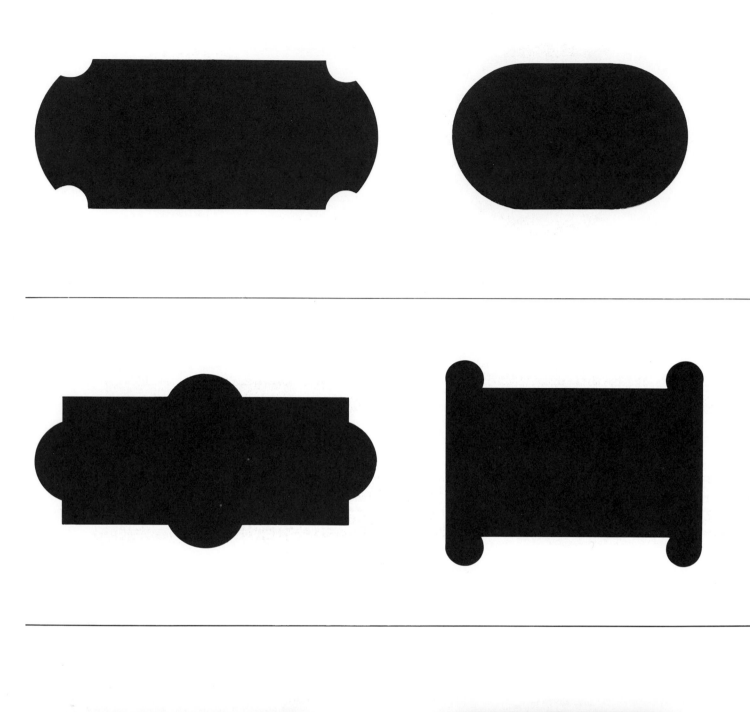

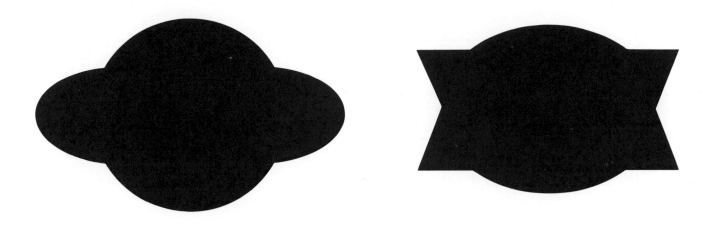

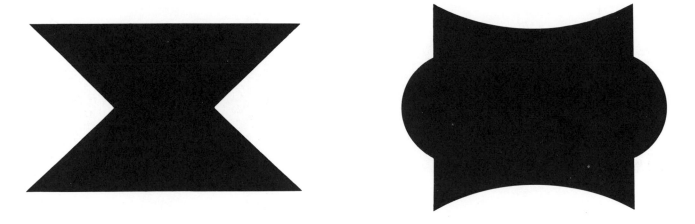

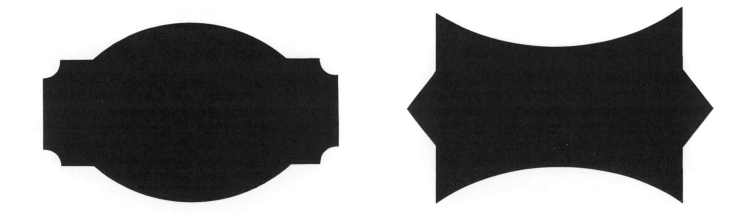

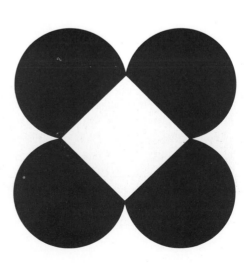

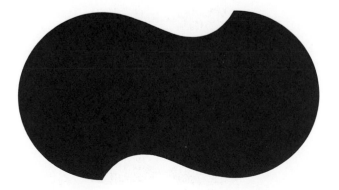

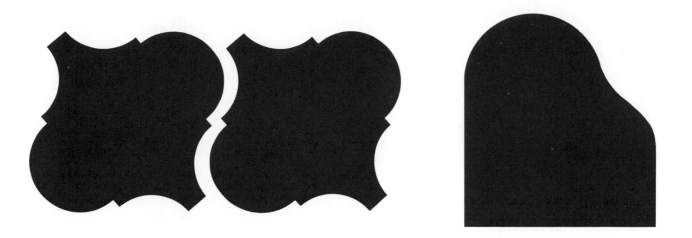

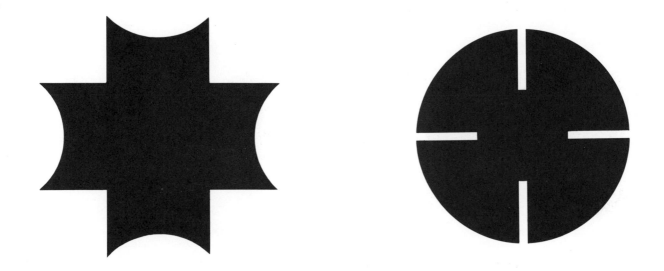

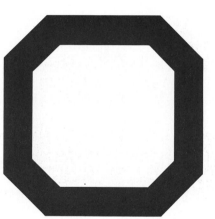

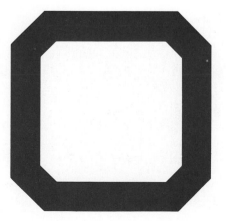

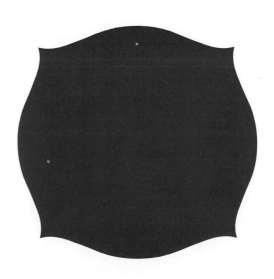

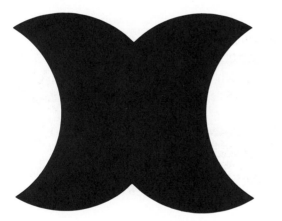

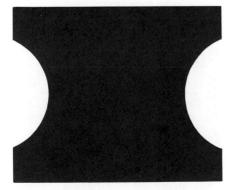

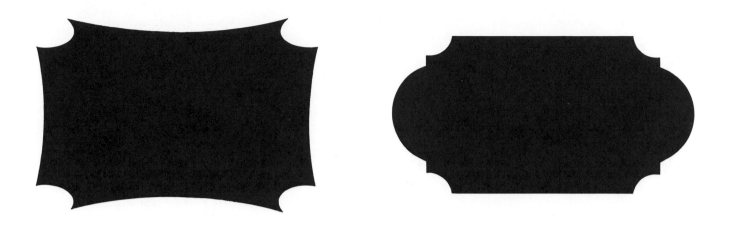

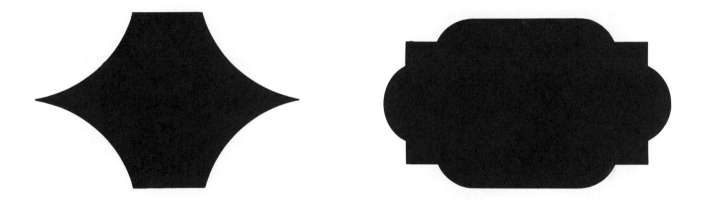

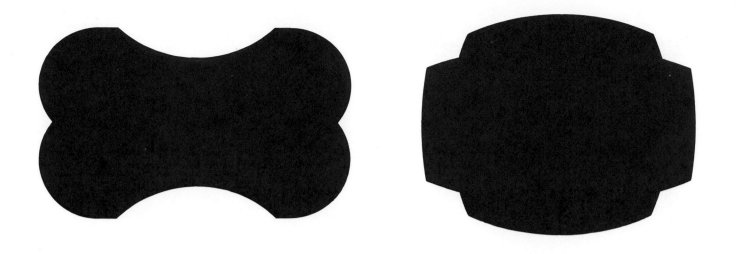

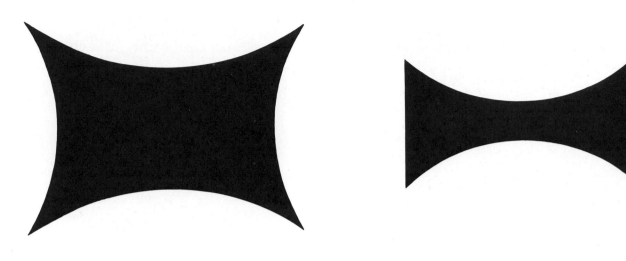

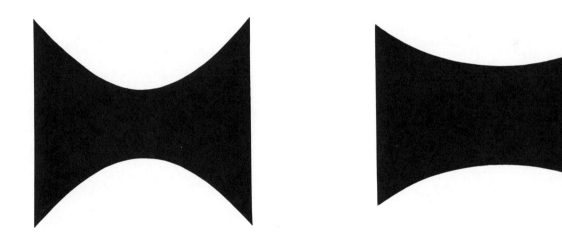

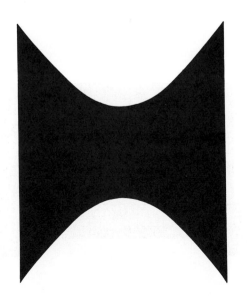

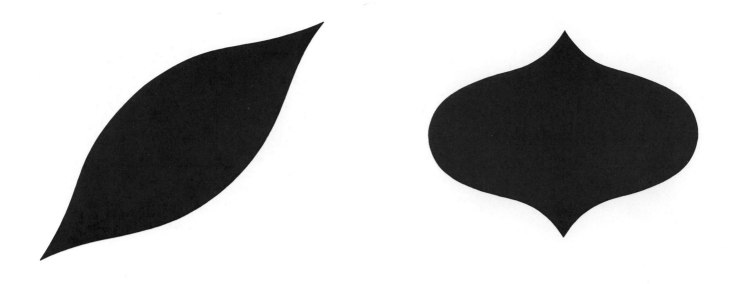

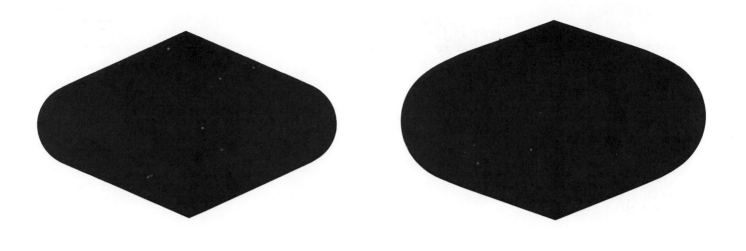

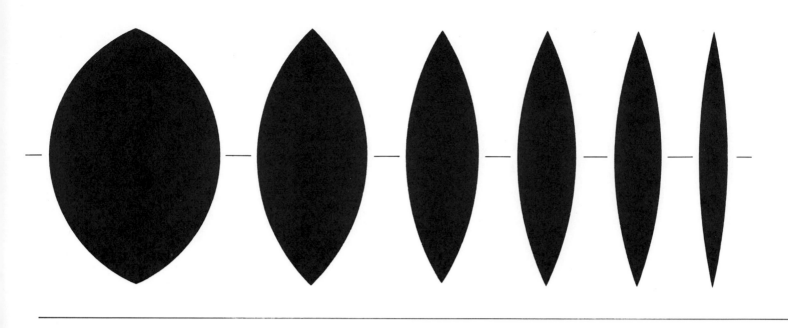

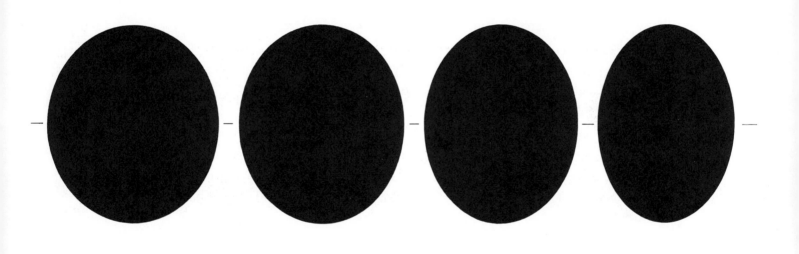

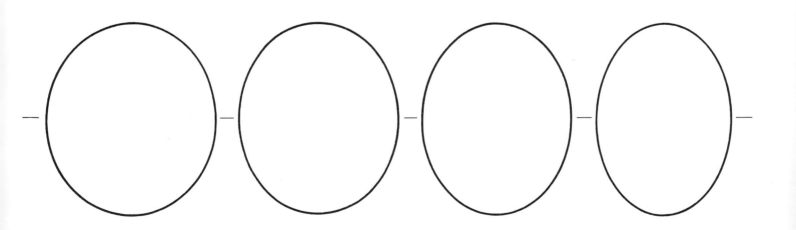

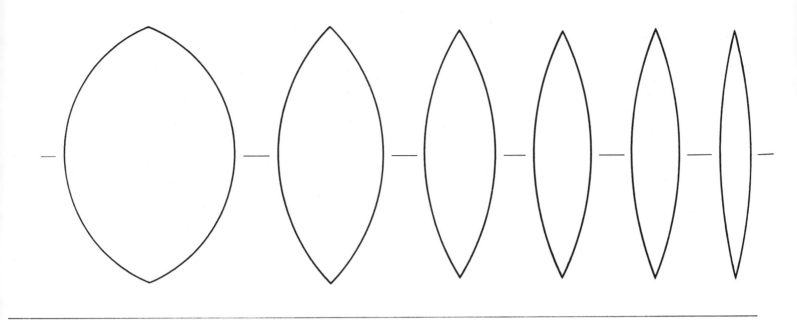

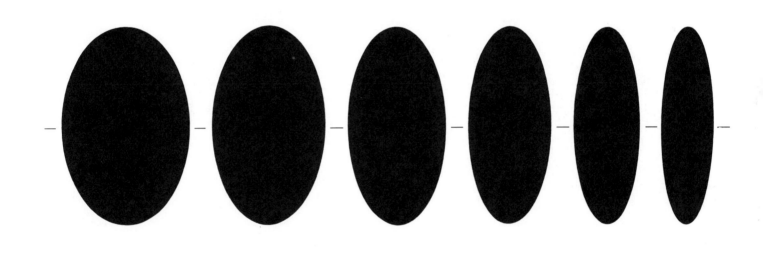

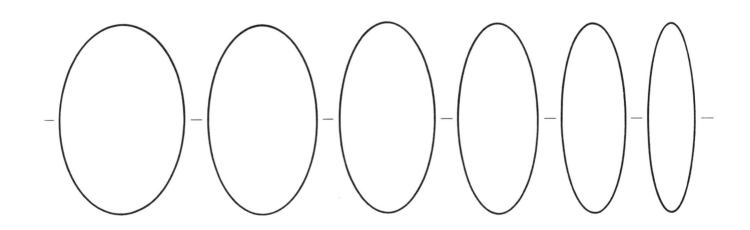

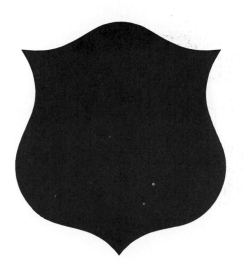

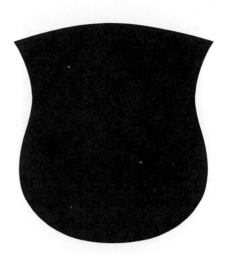

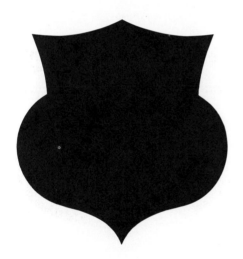

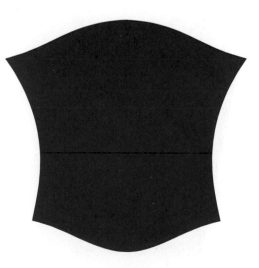

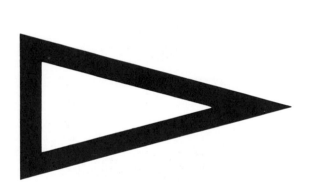

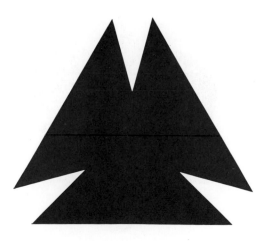

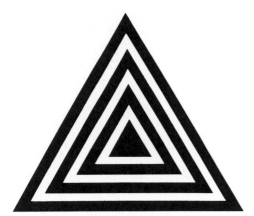

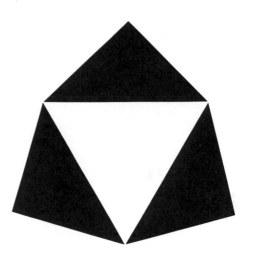